CAMBRIDGE ENGLISH QUALIFICATIONS

Practice Tests
A2 Flyers

• PETRINA CLIFF •

Four practice tests

OXFORD
UNIVERSITY PRESS

OXFORD
UNIVERSITY PRESS

Great Clarendon Street, Oxford, OX2 6DP, United Kingdom

Oxford University Press is a department of the University of Oxford.
It furthers the University's objective of excellence in research, scholarship,
and education by publishing worldwide. Oxford is a registered trade
mark of Oxford University Press in the UK and in certain other countries

© Oxford University Press 2018

The moral rights of the author have been asserted

First published in 2018

2023

10 9 8 7 6

ISBN: 978 0 19 404267 3	Cambridge English Qualifications A2 Flyers Practice Tests Pack
ISBN: 978 0 19 404268 0	Cambridge English Qualifications A2 Flyers Practice Tests Student Book
ISBN: 978 0 19 404270 3	Cambridge English Qualifications A2 Flyers Practice Tests Audio access card
ISBN: 978 0 19 404269 7	Cambridge English Qualifications Practice Tests Audio

Printed in China

This book is printed on paper from certified and well-managed sources

ACKNOWLEDGEMENTS

Back cover photograph: Oxford University Press building/David Fisher

Commissioned illustrations by: John Haslem pp.4, 8, 9, 10, 12, 13, 14, 21, 22, 24, 26, 30, 31, 32, 34, 35, 36, 44, 46, 48, 52, 53, 54, 56, 57, 58, 65, 66, 68, 70, 74, 75, 76, 78, 79, 80, 87, 88, 90; Mark Ruffle pp.6, 7, 16, 18, 20, 23, 28, 29, 38, 40, 42, 45, 50, 51, 60, 62, 64, 67, 72, 73, 82, 84, 86, 89; Gustavo Mazali/Beehive Illustration pp.43

Contents

Part 1

– 5 questions –

Listen and draw lines. There is one example.

David   Bill   Jane

Jill   Sam   Betty   Paul

Part 2

– 5 questions –

Listen and write. There is one example.

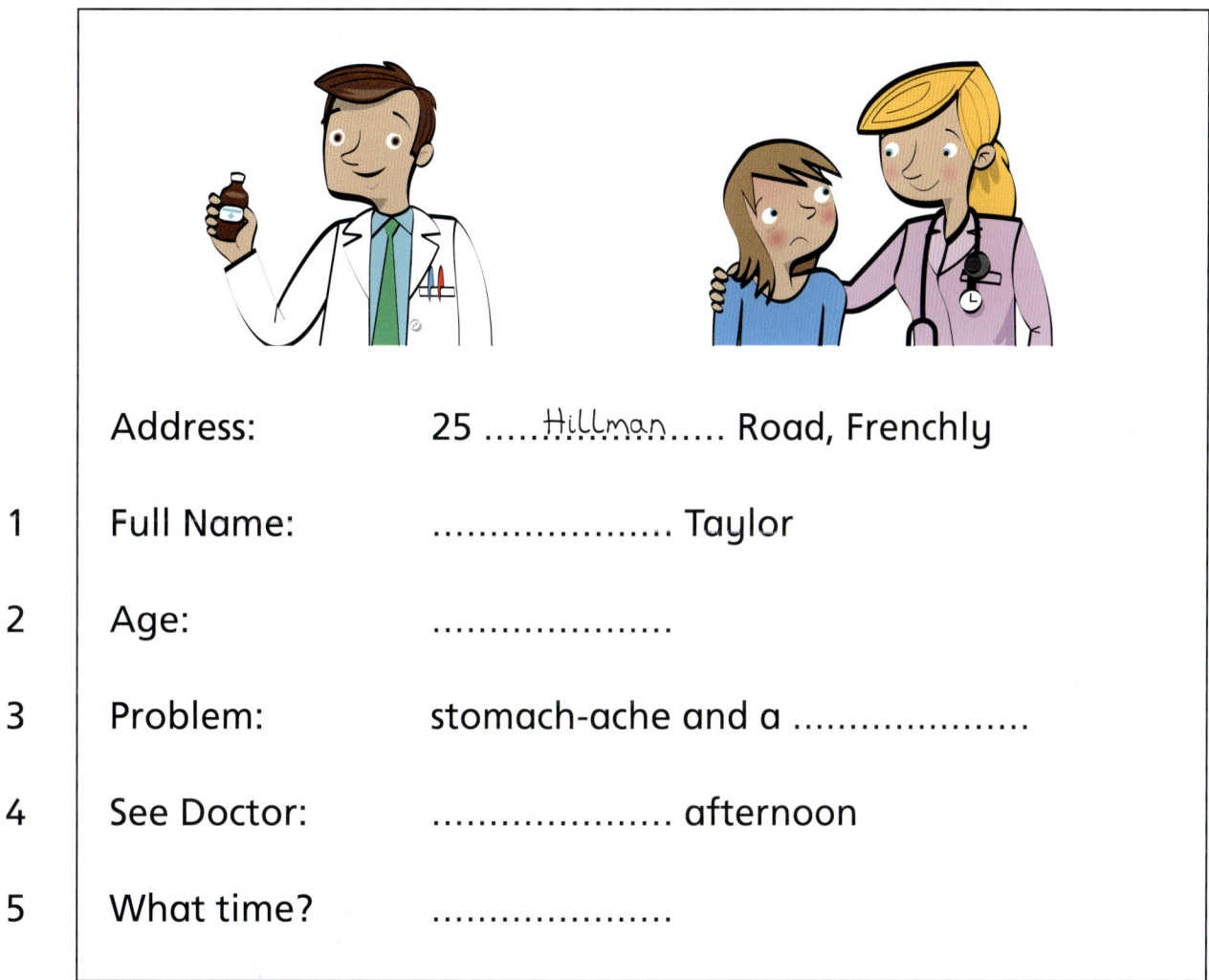

	Address:	25 .....Hillman..... Road, Frenchly
1	Full Name:	.... Taylor
2	Age:	....
3	Problem:	stomach-ache and a ....
4	See Doctor:	.... afternoon
5	What time?	....

Part 3

What are William's friends doing in the school holidays?

Listen and write a letter in each box. There is one example.

	Robert	B
	David	
	Sarah	
	Richard	
	Helen	
	Betty	

A

B

C

D

E

F

G

H

Part 4

– 5 questions –

Listen and tick (✔) the box. There is one example.

Who is Michael's art teacher?

 A ✔

 B ☐

 C ☐

1 Where's the art room at school?

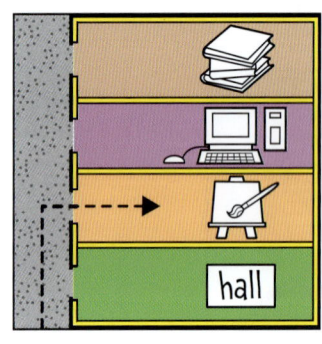 A ☐

 B ☐

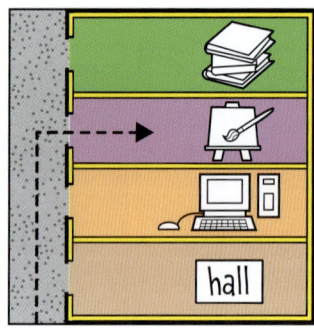 C ☐

2 What time does the club finish?

 A ☐

 B ☐

 C ☐

3 What's Michael going to make at art club?

A ☐

B ☐

C ☐

4 What's Michael going to use to make his toy?

A ☐

B ☐

C ☐

5 Who is Michael making the toy for?

A ☐

B ☐

C ☐

Listen and colour and write. There is one example.

party

My _____

Reading & Writing

Part 1

– 10 questions –

**Look and read. Choose the correct words and write them on the lines.
There is one example.**

a bracelet   shampoo   cushions   pyjamas   a step

This can be brown or white and you use
it when you're making bread or pasta.   .... flour ....

artists

1   You wear these on your feet when
    you want to do sport.   ....

2   Children sit on this when they play in
    the park or in the garden.   ....   soap

3   These are people who work in the
    theatre or on TV.   ....

a tent

4   You use this in the shower when you
    want to wash your hair.   ....   flour

5   This is like a small necklace. You wear
    it on your arm.   ....

6   Chocolates and sweets are made with
    this. It tastes good but it can give you
    toothache.   ....

sugar

7   People sleep in this when they go camping
    by the sea or in the countryside.   ....   a swing

8   You find these on an armchair or sofa.
    They're very nice to sit on.   ....

9   These people need to be very good at
    drawing and painting pictures.   ....   trainers

actors

10 A lot of people wear these when they
    go to bed.   ....

astronauts   a costume

Part 2

– 5 questions –

Holly is talking to her friend, Katy. What does Katy say?

Read the conversation and choose the best answer. Write a letter (A–H) for each answer.

You do not need to use all the letters. There is one example.

Example

Holly: So where have you been?

Katy: ....F..........

Questions

1 Holly: Did you buy anything nice?

Katy: ....

2 Holly: Let's see them then.

Katy: ....

3 Holly: They're lovely! Where did you get them?

Katy: ....

4 Holly: Oh, I'd like to go there!

Katy: ....

5 Holly: That'd be great, but do you want to go again so soon?

Katy: ....

A   Here they are. Do you like them?

B   Oh, I don't mind. Let's do it!

C   From a little shop next to the bank.

D   Well, I got a bracelet from that shop
    you like.

E   Yes, I think you would!

F   Oh, just shopping in town.   **(Example)**

G   Only a pair of pyjamas and a T-shirt.

H   Well, shall we go tomorrow?

Part 3

Read the story. Choose a word from the box. Write the correct word next to numbers 1–5. There is one example.

example				
fire	stamp	thanked	envelope	smelt
believed	corner	front	happened	hole

My name's Oliver. One day I was walking home when I saw a
........fire........ in the downstairs window of an enormous house. I
went to the (**1**) .... door and shouted loudly but nobody
came. I had my phone with me so I phoned and told someone
about the fire. After about five minutes, I heard the noise of an
engine. Then a fire engine with blue lights on the top came round
the (**2**) .... very fast. It was a bit frightening. Suddenly
firefighters were running everywhere, throwing water on the fire.
That was exciting! And soon everything was all right again.

I went into the house with the firefighters. The kitchen was badly
burnt and it (**3**) .... terrible but the other rooms in the
house were fine. Then a man appeared at the bottom of the stairs.
I knew him! He was a famous singer but he was also the man who

lived in the enormous house. He **(4)** .... me very much and asked me for my name and address. Then, two days later, a letter arrived for me. Inside the **(5)** .... there were two tickets for a concert that the man was singing in. I thought that was amazing!

(6) Now choose the best name for the story.

Tick one box.

Oliver gets a lovely surprise ☐

Oliver explores an empty house ☐

Oliver chats to firefighters ☐

Part 4

Read the text. Choose the right words and write them on the lines.

What can robots do?

Example   Robots ....aren't....... just children's toys. Robots can
1   do many things to help us with .... work.
           People invent robots to do all kinds of boring jobs.
           In some factories, for example, they can put sweets
2   carefully into boxes while in .... factories
           they make cars with no help at all!

3   People also design robots .... help us
           understand as much as we can about science. Some
4   robots .... left Earth and been to the moon
           to get rocks for us to study. They also visit other
5   planets .... people can't go.

           An 'android' is a robot which looks like a person.
6   Asimo is the name .... one android robot.
7   It can't feel happy or sad, ... it can walk,
           sit down and stand up. It climbs up and down steps
           too. In this way, it acts like a real person. But can it
8   think? Well, yes, but only .... people give
           it information first. It can't chat with you or
9   .... your homework for you. Not at the
           moment. But robot designers think that one day this
10   .... happen!

Example	don't	isn't	aren't
1	his	our	their
2	other	much	every
3	to	for	by
4	has	have	having
5	what	why	where
6	of	on	at
7	so	but	or
8	if	so	then
9	do	doing	did
10	might	won't	shall

Part 5

– 7 questions –

Look at the picture and read the story. Write some words to complete the sentences about the story. You can use 1, 2, 3 or 4 words.

A bad day at work

My name's Frank and my job is painting things, usually houses. It can be a difficult job when the weather's cold or foggy, because I often have to work outside. Yesterday I went to paint a house for a woman called Mrs Hill, but when I arrived at the house there was no-one there. I decided to start painting because Mrs Hill wanted me to finish it in two days and that really wasn't enough time.

At midday I stopped for lunch and went to a litte café round the corner. I wanted a burger and chips. That's my favourite meal, but they didn't have it, so I had pizza with olives on top instead. It was delicious! I was eating it when a woman phoned me and asked, 'Where are you?' I answered 'I'm having my lunch!' I was surprised because she was very unfriendly and she didn't say she was pleased with my hard work.

At two o'clock I went back to the house but there was still no-one there! Then a woman appeared outside the house next door. She was waiting on a step there. She looked very angry so I asked 'What's the matter?'. She said 'I'm waiting for a man to paint my house. He's really late! He said he'd come this morning but he hasn't arrived yet.' 'What's your name?' I asked. 'Mrs Hill' she said! I was working at the wrong house! I quickly collected all my paint and brushes and disappeared!

Examples

Frank's job isn't easy when the ....weather.......... is bad.

Yesterday Frank ......went to paint...... Mrs Hill's house.

Questions

1 When Frank arrived at the house .... was at home.

2 Frank wanted to start work because he only had .... to do the job.

3 Frank ate .... for lunch.

4 Frank thought the woman sounded .... on the phone.

5 When Frank saw the woman, she was standing on a .... outside her house.

6 The woman explained that the man who was coming to work for her was very ....

7 Bill suddenly understood his mistake. He was painting ....

Part 6

– 5 questions –

Read the diary and write the missing words. Write one word on each line.

Thursday 22ⁿᵈ June

Example Today was a horrible day! ....This........ morning I

1 went to the dentist and he .... at my teeth.
He said there was a hole in one of them. I thought he

2 was very unkind. When he finished, ...
mouth was really sore. Then I cycled to school. I had a

3 geography lesson. We're .... a project
about the ocean, but I'm not really interested. Then,

4 this evening, I wanted to go to a concert ....
my friends. My favourite group's playing pop and rock
music in town. But Mum said

5 I .... to stay at home and do my homework
instead. So at the moment I'm by myself in my room
and I'm bored. I hope tomorrow's better!

Sarah

Part 7

– 1 question –

Look at the three pictures. Write about this story. Write 20 or more words

....
....
....
....
....
....

Speaking

Find the Differences

Candidate's copy

Examiner's copy

Information Exchange

Examiner's copy

Emma's DVD	
Name	?
Who / gave	?
What / about	?
When / watch	?
Exciting / boring	?

William's DVD	
Name	Island Adventure
Who / gave	uncle
What / about	three pirates
When / watch	last week
Exciting / boring	exciting

Candidate's copy

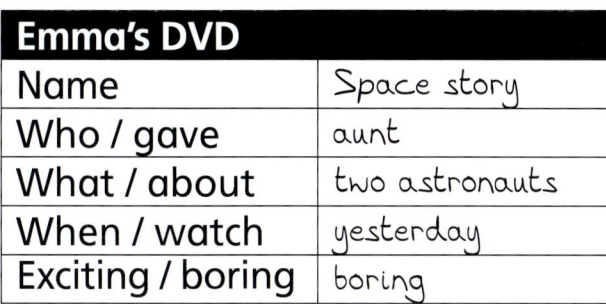

Emma's DVD	
Name	Space story
Who / gave	aunt
What / about	two astronauts
When / watch	yesterday
Exciting / boring	boring

William's DVD	
Name	?
Who / gave	?
What / about	?
When / watch	?
Exciting / boring	?

Picture Story: Jim's new hobby

Jim

Part 1

– 5 questions –

Listen and draw lines. There is one example.

Fred   Lucy   Robert

William   Sally   Katy   Paul

Part 2

– 5 questions –

Listen and write. There is one example.

History Homework

Talk to an old person you know. Find out the answers.

	Age:	.............86.........
1	Name:	.... Smith (my grandfather)
2	Lived where?	.... in south London (only two bedrooms)
3	Family:	five .... and parents
4	First job:	....
5	Hobbies:	driving expensive cars looking at ....

Part 3

– 5 questions –

Where did Mrs Black take the pictures of these people?

Listen and write a letter in each box. There is one example.

Aunt Pat [E]

Dad [ ]

Uncle Fred [ ]

Mum [ ]

Sue [ ]

Alex [ ]

A

B

C

D

E

F

G

H

Part 4

– 5 questions –

Listen and tick (✔) the box. There is one example.

What's Jane going to study next year?

A ☐ B ✔ C ☐

1   Which is Jane's room?

A ☐ B ☐ C ☐

2   Which girl has Jane already met?

A ☐ B ☐ C ☐

3 Which suitcase is Jane going to take?

A ☐

B ☐

C ☐

4 When is Jane going to college?

A ☐

B ☐

C ☐

5 What's Jane going to do this evening?

A ☐

B ☐

C ☐

Part 5

– 5 questions –

Listen and colour and write. There is one example.

_____ adventure

holidays

_____ adventure

Reading & Writing

Part 1

– 10 questions –

Look and read. Choose the correct words and write them on the lines. There is one example.

an octopus   meetings   a bandage   dinosaurs   a festival

a tour

x-rays

a quiz

fur

	You should go and see this person if you have toothache.	.....a dentist.....
1	Some animals have this because they need to be warm in the winter.	....
2	Businessmen and businesswomen work at their desks in these rooms.	....
3	This is a competition. People have to answer questions.	....
4	This creature lives in the ocean and has eight legs.	....
5	If you fall over, a doctor might put this around your knee, for example.	....
6	A great day where people dance, sing and have fun together.	....
7	A bird uses these when it wants to fly.	....
8	This can be a game or a problem you find in magazines and comics.	....
9	These are photographs that doctors take of the inside of people's bodies.	....
10	This is a very slow animal, which has a shell on its back.	....

a puzzle

wings

offices

a toe

a tortoise   a dentist

Part 2

– 5 questions –

Richard is talking to his teacher, Mrs White. What does Mrs White say?

Read the conversation and choose the best answer. Write a letter (A–H) for each answer.

You do not need to use all the letters. There is one example.

Example

Richard:	Hello Mrs White!	
Mrs White:	..............D.............	

Questions

1 Richard: Oh, I'm really sorry but I couldn't do it at the weekend! I was ill.

Mrs White: ....

2 Richard: I know it's late, and I'll do it tonight, Mrs White, I promise!

Mrs White: ....

3 Richard: Oh yes, I thought that was very difficult!

Mrs White: ....

4 Richard: Oh, but I've got football in the gym, Mrs White!

Mrs White: ....

5 Richard: Could I do it later perhaps?

Mrs White: ....

A I'm sorry but, you can't, Jack!

B I'm afraid you'll have to miss that.

C Yes, well, I'm sorry but I want you to do it again this lunch time.

D Oh, Jack! Can I have a word about your homework please?   **(Example)**

E OK Jack. But I also want to talk about the work you did for me yesterday!

F But it's Thursday now Jack!

G Oh, I'm pleased you're feeling better.

H Yes, well you won't forget this time, will you?

Part 3

– 6 questions –

Read the story. Choose a word from the box. Write the correct word next to numbers 1–5. There is one example.

example				
climbing	steps	appeared	yourself	hole
surprise	myself	knee	explored	stones

One evening in summer, I was .....climbing..... in the mountains with my older brother George. We were crossing a stream when I fell over and hurt my **(1)** .... George looked at our map, but he couldn't find out where we were. There was a castle not far away, so we decided to go there and ask for help. We walked up to the enormous door together. It was open.

It was dark and frightening inside the castle. Suddenly, from nowhere, an old woman **(2)** .... She was wearing a black dress. She didn't say anything but she started to walk along the hall away from us. My brother said 'Don't go with her David!' but I wasn't listening. I followed her up some **(3)** .... At the top there was another door, not as big as the first one. The woman opened it and I had a huge **(4)** .... There, in front of me, was a room full of sweets! I went inside and tried to touch them but

36

they disappeared. Suddenly the door closed behind me. I was by
(5) .... !

Then I heard someone in the room. It was George. 'Wake up David!
You'll be late for school!' he said.

(6) **Now choose the best name for the story.**

Tick one box.

The bad dream ☐

The empty castle ☐

The brave woman ☐

Part 4

– 10 questions –

Read the text. Choose the right words and write them on the lines.

Come to London

Example

There are many famous places ....in......... London.
The most famous, perhaps, is Buckingham Palace

1
.... all the kings and queens from history
have lived there. Tower Bridge is over a hundred

2
years old and you .... see it from one of
the boats on the River Thames.

3
London .... lots of things for families to do

4
together. .... you want to go shopping,
Harrods is London's most famous store but it's very
expensive. You'll find that markets sell some very nice

5
things and are .... cheaper. Then, for a
great view, take a lift to the top of the Shard,

6
.... is London's tallest skyscraper.

What about food? There are many restaurants in

7
London, ... the Rainforest Café is amazing.
You can get delicious burgers and pizzas there, and

8
when you go inside you .... see jungle
creatures all around you. In summer it's great to

9
have.................... picnic in one of London's parks,
and when it's rainy, there are lots of different

10
theatres where you can .... famous actors
on stage.

Example	in	at	to
1	when	because	while
2	can	like	want
3	is	has	gives
4	Before	Then	If
5	very	much	most
6	what	that	which
7	but	so	or
8	would	have	will
9	a	an	the
10	watching	watch	watched

Part 5

– 7 questions –

Look at the picture and read the story. Write some words to complete the sentences about the story. You can use 1, 2, 3 or 4 words.

Trip to the museum

My name's Harry. Last week my teacher took our class to The Museum of Science. It's a huge building in the city. We went by bus because it wasn't as expensive as the train. Before we went inside, the teacher gave us a map of the museum and said 'It's half past nine now. Come and find me here as half past eleven. And don't be late!' I didn't have a watch but my friend, Oliver, did. We went to explore.

There were lots of exciting things everywhere. I thought the information about racing cars was really interesting. I found a quiz about planets and wanted to do it with Oliver but he wasn't interested at all. He looked at his map and saw that there were some models of spaceships in the basement so we went and found them. They were amazing! But the best thing at the museum was an enormous rocket. You could go inside it! Then we went into the museum shop. I asked Oliver if I could borrow some money because I didn't have any with me. We couldn't decide what to buy. In the end I got a ruler for my brother with a picture of an astronaut on it and Oliver got a fan for his little sister.

Then Oliver looked at his watch. We were late! We ran to the exit and looked for our teacher. He wasn't there. Suddenly we saw the bus. All our classmates were looking through the window and laughing and waving. But our teacher was standing in front of it and he wasn't laughing!

Examples

Harry's teacher took his class to a place in ....the city.......... called The Museum of Science.

They travelled there by bus because it wasn't .....as expensive as..... going by train.

Questions

1 The teacher told the children to meet him again at
   ....

2 Oliver thought that the .... was a bit boring.

3 The boys decided to go to the basement because there were
   .... there.

4 Harry enjoyed seeing the .... most.

5 Harry needed to .... because he wanted to get
   something from the museum shop.

6 Harry was pleased with his brother's present because there was a
   .... on it.

7 The boys found that their........................... were already on
   the bus!

Part 6

– 5 questions –

Read the diary and write the missing words. Write one word on each line.

	Dear Grandma,
Example	Today I've been ....to.......... my piano lesson. I
1	have lessons with a teacher .... lives
	near our house. It went really well and she says
2	I'm much better .... I was. I was really
3	pleased and I'm .... to do more practice
	now. It's not long until the weekend and Dad's got
4	us some tickets for a football match ....
	the stadium in town. I'm excited about that
5	.... my favourite team's playing! Well, I'm
	tired now. Time for bed!
	Love,
	Sue

Part 7

– 1 question –

Look at the three pictures. Write about this story. Write 20 or more words

....

....

....

....

....

....

Speaking

Find the Differences

44

Information Exchange

Examiner's copy

Frank's holiday	
Where	?
Weather good	?
How long	?
What / do	?
Who / with	?

Sophia's holiday	
Where	sea
Weather good	yes – sunny
How long	two weeks
What / do	swimming
Who / with	family

Candidate's copy

Frank's holiday	
Where	mountains
Weather good	no – foggy
How long	ten days
What / do	cycling
Who / with	school friends

Sophia's holiday	
Where	?
Weather good	?
How long	?
What / do	?
Who / with	?

Picture Story : Mrs Brown forgets her handbag

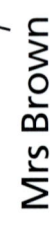

Mrs Brown

Part 1

– 5 questions –

Listen and draw lines. There is one example.

Sophia Frank Oliver

Helen Peter Mary Robert

Part 2

– 5 questions –

Listen and write. There is one example.

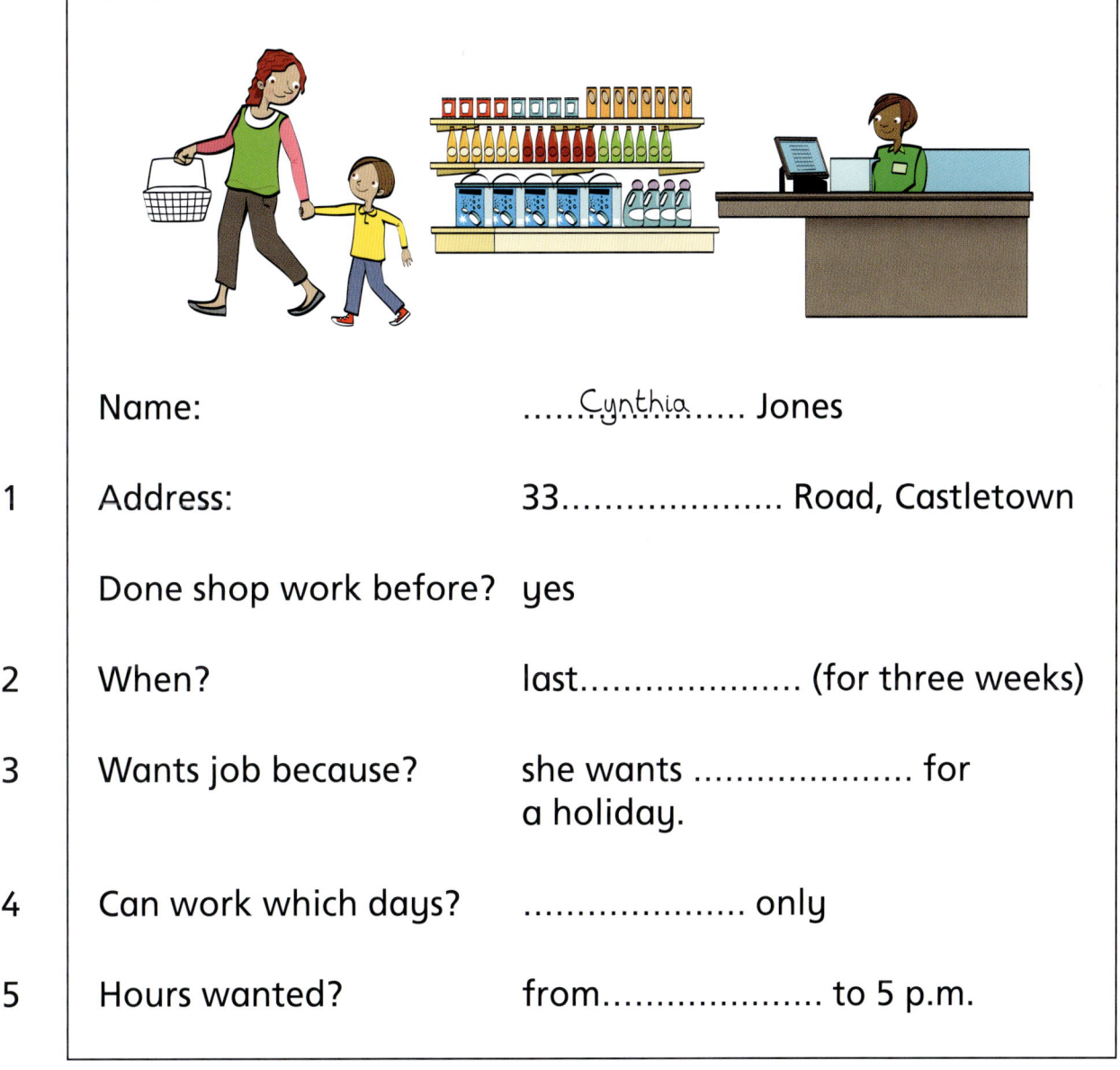

	Name:	......Cynthia...... Jones
1	Address:	33.................... Road, Castletown
	Done shop work before?	yes
2	When?	last.................... (for three weeks)
3	Wants job because?	she wants .... for a holiday.
4	Can work which days?	.... only
5	Hours wanted?	from.................... to 5 p.m.

Part 3

– 5 questions –

Where did Mrs Banks buy the things for the party?

Listen and write a letter in each box. There is one example.

	shoes	D
	CDs	
	pizzas	
	sweets	
	cake	
	diaries	

A

B

C

D

E

F

G

H

Part 4

– 5 questions –

Listen and tick (✔) the box. There is one example.

What time did Richard see the doctor?

 A ☐

 B ✔

 C ☐

1   What did the doctor tell Richard to do?

 A ☐

 B ☐

 C ☐

2   What's the matter with Richard now?

 A ☐

 B ☐

 C ☐

3   What does Richard ask his mother for?

A ☐

B ☐

C ☐

4   What homework has Richard got to do?

A ☐

B ☐

C ☐

5   When is Richard going to go back to school?

A ☐

B ☐

C ☐

Part 5

– 5 questions –

Listen and colour and write. There is one example.

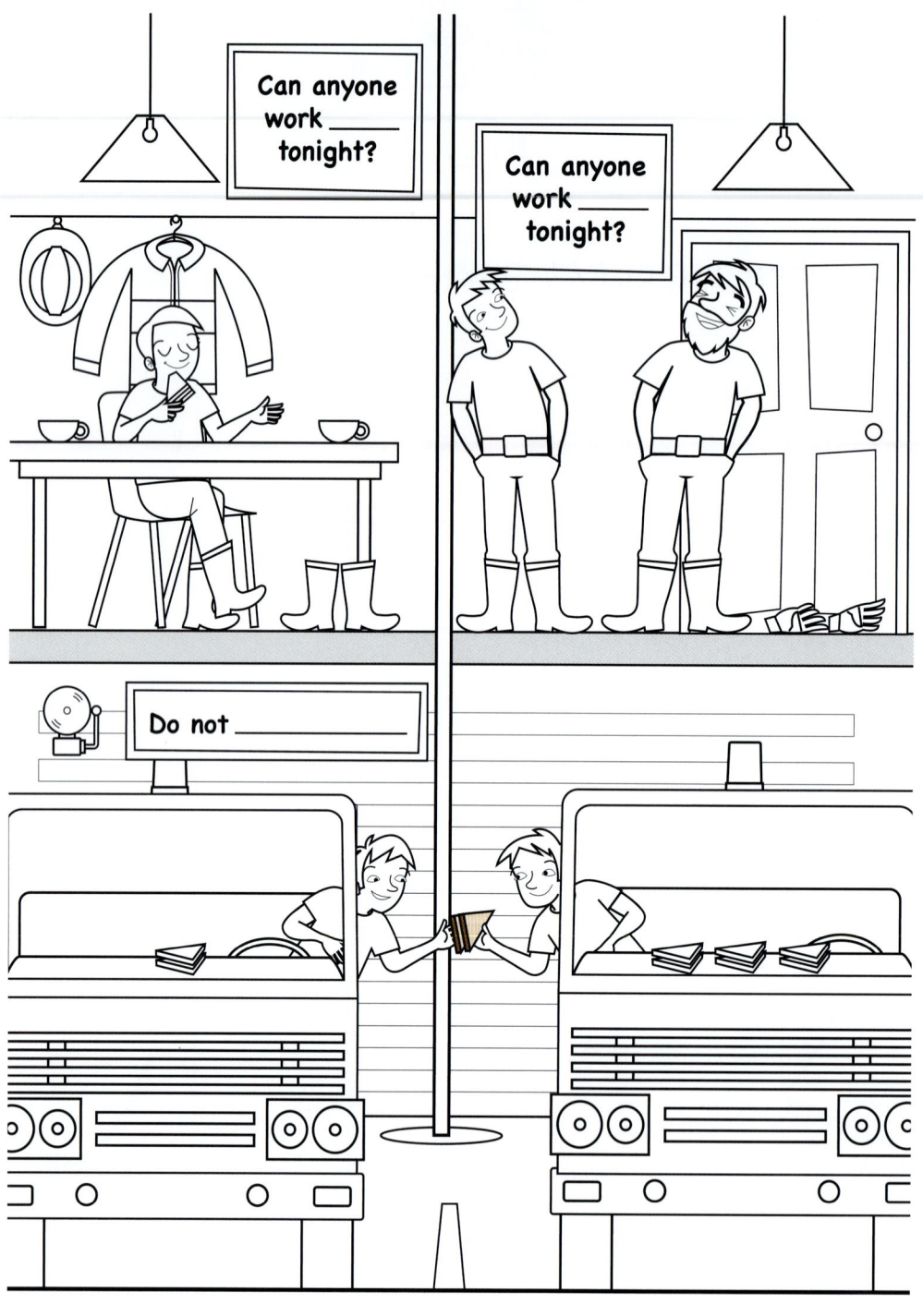

Reading & Writing

Part 1

– 10 questions –

**Look and read. Choose the correct words and write them on the lines.
There is one example.**

a spaceship   a journey   pockets   a platform   motorways

When you don't want them, you throw
paper and other things in these. ....bins.........

bins   tyres

1 One day we might travel to stars and
other planets in one of these. ....

2 You stand on this while you're waiting
to catch your train. ....

3 This is often blue in the day and at night
you can see the moon and stars here. ....

scissors   a gym

4 There are four of these round car
wheels. They're black. ....

5 These are often made of wood and you
put books, photographs and other
things on them. ....

sky   screens

6 These are very tall buildings, often in
the centre of towns and cities. ....

7 You can't see this but animals and plants
need it to live, and we do too. ....

8 Cars and trucks travel fast along these
huge roads. ....

shelves   air

9 Coats and trousers often have these and
you can put things in them. ....

10 People go to this building when they
want to do sport. ....

skyscrapers   railway

Part 2

David is talking to his friend, Paul. What does Paul say?

Read the conversation and choose the best answer. Write a letter (A–H) for each answer.

You do not need to use all the letters. There is one example.

Example

	David:	I'm going to go on holiday tomorrow.
	Paul:	..............F..............

Questions

1 David: I'm going to go skiing in the mountains!

   Paul: ....

2 David: My best friend and his family.

   Paul: ....

3 David: Once, but that was years ago.

   Paul: ....

4 David: I'm not sure but I'll soon find out!

   Paul: ....

5 David: Thanks. Are you going to do anything nice?

   Paul: ....

A I'm just staying at home with my family, but it'll be OK.

B Well I hope you have a great time!

C That sounds a bit dangerous! Why?

D I think I'd like that!

E Great! And have you ever been before?

F You must be excited! Where are you going to go? **(Example)**

G That sounds fun. Who with?

H Do you think you'll remember how to do it?

Part 3

– 6 questions –

Read the story. Choose a word from the box. Write the correct word next to numbers 1–5. There is one example.

example				
time	journeys	chat	cycle	stay
homework	gym	laughed	bicycles	racing

My name's Harry. Today I had a terrible day. It all started this morning. It was ....time........ to go to school but my brother, William, wasn't ready. He couldn't find his English (**1**) .... There was a big search for it and I found it under the sofa. And then Mum said she hadn't got her car keys. We looked for them but we couldn't find them anywhere. We have to be at school at nine o'clock and it was already half past eight. The school isn't near our house, but we decided to (**2**) .... there.

After lunch, my classmates did sport in the (**3**) .... , while I stayed in class by myself and did maths instead. I wasn't very pleased about that! At the end of the day we rode our (**4**) .... home again. When we got there we were really tired. Then suddenly William said 'Look Harry!' and he

pointed to the car. There, in the car door, were the keys. We all
(5) .... until Mum said quietly, 'I can't find the keys to the
house now!'

(6) Now choose the best name for the story.

   Tick one box.

   Mum's lost keys   ☐

   Harry's frightening day   ☐

   William's bad mistake   ☐

Part 4

– 10 questions –

Read the text. Choose the right words and write them on the lines.

What do journalists do?

Example

Journalists do ....many....... different things at work. Here is an idea of some of the things journalists do.

1 Before they .... write anything, journalists go and meet people and ask lots of questions

2 .... they need to find out information before they write their stories. Journalists will sometimes pay to have good wifi so that they know they can send information back to newspaper offices

3 .... News stories are usually quite short

4 and give the .... important information

5 about things that .... just happened. Journalists often work with photographers

6 .... take pictures which help to tell the the stories.

When they write their stories, journalists use different computer programs to make sure that

7 there aren't .... mistakes in their work.

8 They must be sure that .... is correct before the stories go into newspapers. It isn't easy to

9 be a journalist but it's .... boring! It's a job with lots of different surprises every day.

10 .... you interested in this work?

Example	other	more	many
1	shall	can	could
2	but	when	because
3	quick	quicker	quickly
4	best	most	much
5	are	has	have
6	who	how	what
7	any	some	lots
8	something	everything	nothing
9	always	often	never
10	Do	is	Are

Part 5

– 7 questions –

Look at the picture and read the story. Write some words to complete the sentences about the story. You can use 1, 2, 3 or 4 words.

Going to the airport

My name's Nick. Last summer I went on holiday with my parents and my sister, Holly. We got up early in the morning because we were going by plane. We packed our suitcases the night before. The next morning Dad woke us all at six o'clock! Holly and I ate some cereal and yoghurt, then we were ready to go. We were really excited!

Dad decided to take the motorway to the airport. We were worried about the time because there were so many cars in front of us so Dad was driving very slowly. It was foggy too and Dad couldn't see very well at all. Suddenly, there was a loud noise as Dad hit the car in front of us. We weren't going fast so it wasn't a bad accident but the man in the other car was very unkind and shouted at Dad. That was frightening. He asked Dad for our address and Dad wrote it down for him on some paper. Then Dad started driving again, very carefully!

When we arrived at the airport we were late and Mum said 'We've missed the plane now!' She was very angry too. Poor Dad! But when we got inside the airport Mum found that our plane was still there. She was pleased about that. So we had a sandwich and a drink at the airport café. And we had a really amazing holiday!

Examples

Last summer Nick had a ....holiday.......... with his family.

They put everything in their ....suitcases......... before they went to bed.

Questions

1   The next morning, Nick and his sister got up very early and had .... for breakfast.

2   The journey to the airport was difficult because there was too much traffic on the .... , and the weather was bad.

3   Nick heard .... when his dad had the accident.

4   Nick said it was .... when the man in the other car shouted at his dad.

5   Nick's dad gave the man his .... and then drove to the airport.

6   Nick's mum felt .... when she found that they could still catch their plane.

7   While the family waited for their plane, they decided to have a snack at the ....

Part 6

– 5 questions –

Read the diary and write the missing words. Write one word on each line.

	Dear Emma,
Example	I can't wait ......_until_...... you come and see me
1	next week. We'll .... an amazing time together. I know you're coming by plane so I'll
2	meet you .... the airport with my family.
3	There are .... of different things to do here so I know you won't be bored. On your first
4	day we're .... to go into town to do some shopping. Then there's a huge festival on
5	Wednesday. The .... is very rainy here at the moment, so don't forget to bring your umbrella!
	See you very soon.
	Lots of love,
	Sarah

Part 7

– 1 question –

Look at the three pictures. Write about this story. Write 20 or more words

....
....
....
....
....
....

Speaking

Find the Differences

Candidate's copy

Candidate's copy

Examiner's copy

Information Exchange

Examiner's copy

Robert's restaurant	
Where	?
Who / with	?
Time	?
How / go	?
What / eat	?

Betty's restaurant	
Where	next / stadium
Who / with	friends
Time	8.30
How / go	bus
What / eat	burger / salad

Candidate's copy

Robert's restaurant	
Where	opposite / police station
Who / with	parents
Time	7.30
How / go	car
What / eat	pizza / olives

Betty's restaurant	
Where	?
Who / with	?
Time	?
How / go	?
What / eat	?

Picture Story : The homework and the scissors

Daisy   Harry

Part 1

– 5 questions –

Listen and draw lines. There is one example.

Alex   Jack   Vicky

Emma   Anna   Jim   Harry

Part 2

– 5 questions –

Listen and write. There is one example.

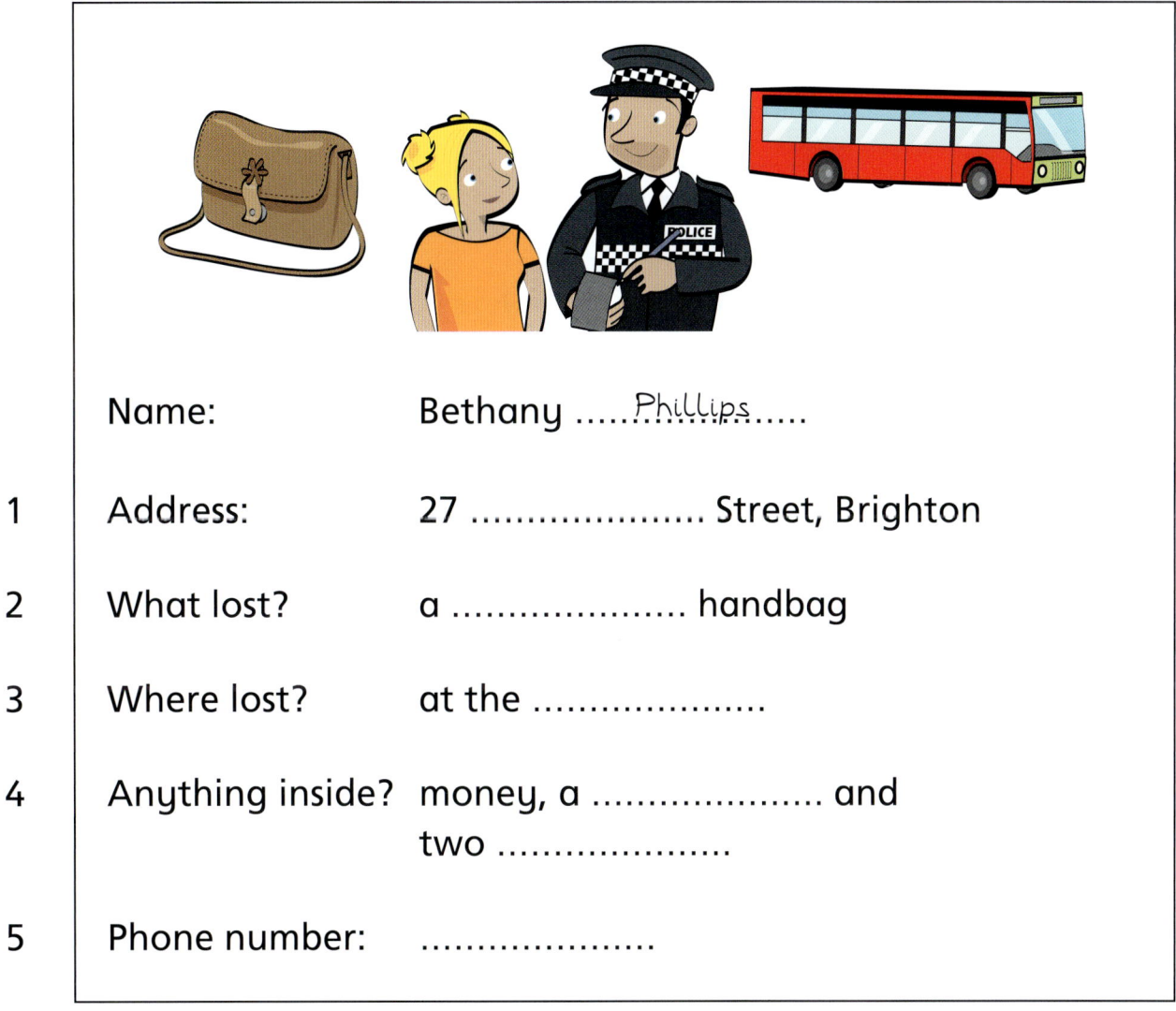

Name: Bethany ......Phillips.....

1   Address: 27 .... Street, Brighton

2   What lost?   a .... handbag

3   Where lost?   at the ....

4   Anything inside?   money, a .... and
                                  two ....

5   Phone number: ....

Part 3

– 5 questions –

Where are the things that Jill has left at her Aunt's house?

Listen and write a letter in each box. There is one example.

	brush	C
	key	
	umbrella	
	belt	
	torch	
	comb	

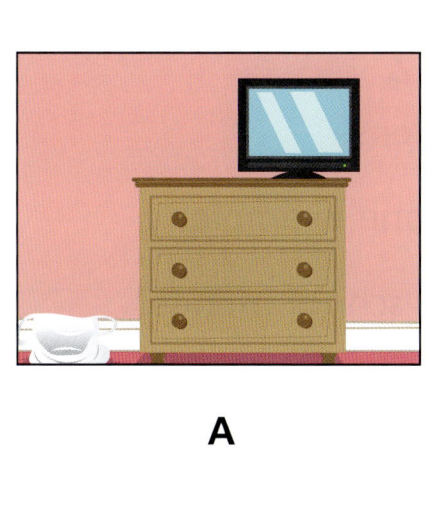

A

B

C

D

E

F

G

H

Part 4

– 5 questions –

Listen and tick (✔) the box. There is one example.

Where's William going to go with his school friends?

A ☐

B ☐

C ✔

1   What has William forgotten to put in his rucksack?

A ☐

B ☐

C ☐

2   What's the weather going to be like?

A ☐

B ☐

C ☐

3   Where's William going to stay?

A ☐

B ☐

C ☐

4   How's William going to get there?

A ☐

B ☐

C ☐

5   What doesn't William want to eat when he's away?

A ☐

B ☐

C ☐

Part 5

– 5 questions –

Listen and colour and write. There is one example.

Reading & Writing

Part 1

– 10 questions –

**Look and read. Choose the correct words and write them on the lines.
There is one example.**

stones   butterflies   deserts   bridges   nests

You can see through this and bottles are sometimes made of it.	.......glass.......
1 People eat this for breakfast. They put milk on it.	....
2 These are in trees and birds make them to live in.	....
3 This is a really delicious red fruit.	....
4 These are strong birds with huge wings. They eat small creatures like rabbits and mice.	....
5 This comes from trees and people make tables, chairs and other things with it.	....
6 These are like small rocks and you find them on roads and in gardens.	....
7 This comes from sheep and we make sweaters and blankets with it.	....
8 You walk over these when you want to cross roads, streams or rivers.	....
9 You make this with milk. People put honey, sugar or fruit in it.	....
10 In children's books, kings and queens might live in one of these buildings.	....

a castle   cereal

wool   a path

eagles   glass

metal   wood

a strawberry   yoghurt

Part 2

– 5 questions –

Emma is talking to her friend, Holly. What does Holly say?

Read the conversation and choose the best answer. Write a letter (A–H) for each answer.

You do not need to use all the letters. There is one example.

Example

	Emma:	Hi Holly. Are you going to Sarah's party?
	Holly:	............C............

Questions

1 Emma: So what are you going to get for her?

   Holly: ....

2 Emma: Don't you think that'll be too expensive?

   Holly: ....

3 Emma: I thought I'd get a game for her new laptop.

   Holly: ....

4 Emma: Tomorrow after school, I think.

   Holly: ....

5 Emma: Yes, OK. I'll meet you outside the gym after lessons.

   Holly: ....

A   That sounds good! Where are you going to get it?

B   Great and perhaps I'll look for a cheaper present!

C   Yes, but I haven't got a present for her yet.   **(Example)**

D   Oh, it might be. What are you getting her then?

E   Well, shall we go together then?

F   I don't know what present to get!

G   I'm not sure. I was thinking about a gold bracelet.

H   Oh, that's a great idea! When are you going to get it?

Part 3

– 6 questions –

Read the story. Choose a word from the box. Write the correct word next to numbers 1–5. There is one example.

example				
sea	enormous	beetles	appeared	nest
stones	hole	disappeared	deep	pond

Last year I was staying with my family in a lovely hotel by the ....sea........ . From our window we could see a small island. Dad wanted to go there so, one afternoon, he decided to borrow a boat from someone at the hotel. We took a picnic and a few blankets and were sailing to the island when, suddenly, it got very foggy. We couldn't see where we were going. The boat hit a rock and **(1)** .... into the water. My sister hurt her elbow when she fell in, but we were all OK.

The water wasn't actually very **(2)** .... , so we got to the island quite easily. We sat on some large stones on the beach and ate our sandwiches, which were still dry because they were in Mum's rucksack. But then a storm came and it started to get dark. We found a **(3)** .... between some rocks. It was a cave, so we went inside. Mum had a torch with her so we could still see. Dad put the blankets on the ground and that's where we slept all night. It was frightening because we could hear strange noises. Mum said it was only (4) .... and other small creatures, which were living there. That didn't really make me feel better!

The next day an (5) .... ship full of people arrived on the island and our adventure was over!

(6) Now choose the best name for the story.

Tick one box.

An interesting island ☐

An exciting adventure ☐

A terrible holiday ☐

Part 4

– 10 questions –

Read the text. Choose the right words and write them on the lines.

The Sahara Desert

Example

The Sahara Desert is the ......biggest...... of 22 deserts and is sometimes called the Sea of Sand. The temperature can be very high, and the land is dry

1 .... it doesn't rain very often.

An 'oasis' is like an enormous pond in the desert. The water in an oasis comes from streams and rivers

2 .... the ground. There are many 'oases' in

3 the Sahara desert but people often .... to travel for many days to find one.

Although life is difficult in the Sahara, a lot of people

4 .... live there. They move from one place to another to find the water they need and use

5 camels to carry .... when they move. Camels have large feet which means that they can

6 walk easily .... the sand and stones.

7 Lots of .... animals live in the Sahara too: snakes, lizards and beetles, for example. These

8 animals get .... of their water from the

9 plants they eat. .... the day small desert creatures look for cool holes in the ground to sleep in and other animals lie under trees. And did you

10 .... that the Sahara is growing every year?

82

Example	big	bigger	biggest
1	but	because	then
2	under	between	into
3	has	have	had
4	still	also	yet
5	nothing	anything	everything
6	over	above	opposite
7	both	another	other
8	many	most	more
9	Until	During	Since
10	know	knew	known

Part 5

– 7 questions –

Look at the picture and read the story. Write some words to complete the sentences about the story. You can use 1, 2, 3 or 4 words.

At the bank

My name's Richard and I'm a photographer. I work for a big newspaper in the city. Yesterday afternoon I was going to the stadium there to take some pictures of famous pop stars. I was walking past the bank and I decided to go in because I needed to get money to buy some lunch later.

But when I was inside I knew something was wrong. There was a man there who had a black sweater on. I couldn't see his face, but he was holding an enormous plastic bag. A woman was putting money into it. I knew then that he was stealing the money so I shouted 'Stop right now!' He turned round and I took his picture. He looked very surprised! He just dropped the money and then, before I could catch him, he ran out of the bank. Everyone said I was very brave and they thanked me.

Then a police officer arrived and had a chat with me. Someone told him that I had a photograph of the man. But the police officer asked, 'Why did you take his picture?' and said it was a dangerous thing to do. Then he said he had to take my camera to the police station and he'd let me know when I could go and collect it. He was a bit unfriendly actually. I didn't get my photos of famous pop stars that day!

Examples

Richard works as a ...... *photographer* ....

Yesterday he had to go ...... *to the stadium* ..... in the city.

Questions

1   Richard went into the bank because he needed to get money for
    ....

2   Richard saw a man in the bank who was wearing
    ....

3   The man had .... in his hands.

4   The man was .... when Richard took a photo
    of him.

5   Before the man left the bank, he ....

6   The people at the bank told Richard that he was
    ....

7   Richard said that the police officer was ....

Part 6

– 5 questions –

Read the diary and write the missing words. Write one word on each line.

	Hello everyone!
Example	I'm ......*having*...... a great time here with Robert. Yesterday we went to see a football match and I
1	was really pleased because my team .... The score was 5-3! After the match, a man said
2	'hello' to me, but I didn't know .... he was. He was the manager of my team! That was a
3	real surprise. Tomorrow we're .... to go to the swimming pool. The swimming pool's outside and it's lovely there, but it won't be nice
4	.... the weather's bad. Then I'll
5	.... back at school again next Monday. I'm not very happy about that!
	David

Part 7

– 1 question –

Look at the three pictures. Write about this story. Write 20 or more words

....

....

....

....

....

....

Speaking

Find the Differences

Information Exchange

Examiner's copy

Katy's Lesson	
Teacher	?
What subject	?
How long	?
What day	?
What / study today	?

Michael's Lesson	
Teacher	Mrs Green
What subject	Science
How long	one hour
What day	Tuesday
What / study today	engines

Candidate's copy

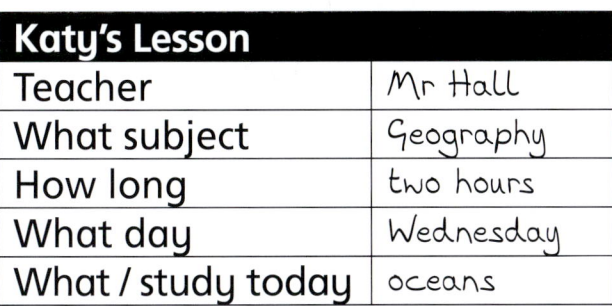

Katy's Lesson	
Teacher	Mr Hall
What subject	Geography
How long	two hours
What day	Wednesday
What / study today	oceans

Michael's Lesson	
Teacher	?
What subject	?
How long	?
What day	?
What / study today	?

Picture Story : The baby and the biscuits

Jane

Sally

Flyers Vocabulary List

Students at this level are also expected to be familiar with all the words in the YLE Starters and Movers Vocabulary List which can be found in the Cambridge YLE Tests handbook.

n = noun	**det** = determiner	**dis** = discourse marker
v = verb	**adv** = adverb	**int** = interjection
adj = adjective	**conj** = conjunction	**excl** = exclamation
prep = preposition	**pron** = pronoun	**poss** = possessive
num = number	**int** = interrogative	

A

a.m. *for time*
across **prep**
act **v**
actor **n**
after **adv + conj**
ago **adv**
agree **v**
air **n**
airport **n**
already **adv**
also **adv**
amazing **adj + excl**
ambulance **n**
anyone **pron**
anything **pron**
anywhere **adv**
appear **v**
April **n**
arrive **v**
art **n**
artist **n**
as ... as ...   **conj**
astronaut **n**
at the moment **prep**
August **n**
autumn **n**
away **adv**

B

bandage **n**
bank **n**
beetle **n**
before **adv + conj**
begin **v**
believe **v**
belt **n**
bicycle **n**
bin **n**
biscuit **n** (US cookie)
bookshop **n**
bored **adj**
borrow **v**
bracelet **n**
brave **adj**
break **v**
bridge **n**
broken **adj**
brush **n + v**
burn **v**
bus stop **n**
business **n**
businessman/woman **n**
butter **n**
butterfly **n**
by myself
by yourself

C

camel **n**
camp **v**
candy **n** (UK sweet(s))
card **n**
castle **n**
cave **n**
century **n**
cereal **n**
chat **v**
cheap **adj**
chemist('s) **n**
chocolate **n**
chopsticks **n**
circus **n**
club **n**
college **n**
comb **n + v**
competition **n**
conversation **n**
cook **n**
cooker **n**
cookie **n** (UK biscuit)
corner **n**
costume **n**
could **v** (for possibility)
creature **n**
cushion **n**
cut **v**
cycle **v**

D

dangerous **adj**
dark **adj**
date **n** (as in time)
dear **adj** (as in Dear Harry)
December **n**
decide **v**
deep **adj**
delicious **adj**
dentist **n**
desert **n**
design **v**
designer **n**
diary **n**
dictionary **n**
dinousaur **n**
disappear **v**
drum **n**
dry **adj**
during **prep**

E

each **det + pron**
eagle **n**
early **adj + adv**
Earth **n**
east **n**
elbow **n**
else **adv**
empty **adj**
end **v**
engine **n**
engineer **n**
enormous **adj**
enough **adj + pron**
enter (a competition) **v**
envelope **n**
environment **n**
ever **adv**
everyone **pron**
everything **pron**

everywhere **adv**
excellent **adj + excl**
excited **adj**
expensive **adj**
explain **v**
explore **v**
extinct **adj**

F

factory **n**
fall **v**
fall over **v**
far **adj + adv**
fast **adj + adv**
February **n**
feel **v**
festival **n**
fetch **v**
a few **det**
(open and close)
 a file **v**
find out **v**
finish **v**
fire **n**
fire engine **n**
fire fighter **n**
fire station **n**
flag **n**
flashlight **n** (UK torch)
flour **n**
fog **n**
foggy **adj**
follow **v**
for **prep of time**
forget **v**
fork **n**
fridge **n**
friendly **adj**
frightening **adj**
front **adj + n**
full **adj**
fun **adj + n**

fur **n**
furry **adj**
future **n**

G

geography **n**
get off **v**
get on **v**
get to **v**
glass **adj**
glove **n**
glue **n + v**
Go away! **excl**
go out **v**
gold **adj + n**
golf **n**
group **n**
grow **v**
guess **n + v**
gym **n**

H

half **adj + n**
happen **v**
hard **adj + adv**
hate **v**
hear **v**
heavy **adj**
high **adj**
hill **n**
history **n**
hole **n**
horrible **adj**
hotel **n**
hour **n**
husband **n**

I

ice **n**
if **conj**
If you want! **excl**

ill **adj**
important **adj**
In a minute! **excl**
insect **n**
instead **adv**
interested **v**
interesting **adj**
into **prep**
invent **v**
invitation **n**

J

jam **n**
January **n**
job **n**
journalist **n**
July **n**
June **n**
just **adv**

K

key **n**
kilometre **n** (US
kilometer)
kind **adj**
knee **n**
knife **n**

L

land **n**
language **n**
late **adj + adv**
later **adv**
leave **v**
left **adj + n** (as in
direction)
let **v**
letter **n** (as in mail)
lie **v** (as in lie down)
light **adj + n**
little **adj**

a little **adv + det**
London **n**
look after **v**
look like **v**
lovely **adj**
low **adj**

M

magazine **n**
manager **n**
March **n**
married **adj**
maths **n** (US math)
May **n** (as in month)
may **v**
meal **n**
mechanic **n**
medicine **n**
meet **v**
meeting **n**
metal **adj + n**
midday **n**
midnight **n**
might **v**
mind **v**
minute **n**
missing **adj**
mix **v**
money **n**
month **n**
motorway **n**
much **adv + det + pron**
museum **n**

N

nest **n**
news **n**
newspaper **n**
next **adj + adv**
No problem! **excl**
noisy **adj**
no-one **pron**

north **n**
November **n**
nowhere **adv**

O

o'clock **adv**
ocean **n**
October **n**
octopus **n**
of course **adv**
office **n**
olives **n**
once **adv**
other **det + pron**
oven **n**
over **adv + prep**

P

p.m. *for time*
paper **adj + n**
past **n + prep**
pepper **n**
perhaps **adv**
photographer **n**
piece **n**
pilot **n**
pizza **n**
planet **n**
plastic **adj + n**
plate **n**
platform **n**
player **n**
pleased **v**
pocket **n**
police officer **n**
police station **n**
poor **adj**
pond **n**
pop music **n**
post **v**
postcard **n**
post office **n**

prefer **v**
problem **n**
program **n**
project **n**
pull **v**
push **v**
puzzle **n**
pyjamas **n**
pyramid **v**

Q

quarter **n**
queen **n**
quiz **n**

R

race **n + v**
racing (car, bike) **n**
ready **adj**
remember **v**
restaurant **n**
rich **adj**
right **adj + n** (as in direction)
ring **n**
rock music **n**
rocket **n**
rucksack **n**

S

salt **n**
same **adj**
science **n**
scissors **n**
score **n + v**
search **n**
secret **n**
sell **v**
send **v**
September **n**
shampoo **n**

shelf **n**
shorts **n**
should **v**
silver **adj + n**
since **prep**
singer **n**
ski **n + v**
sky **n**
skyscraper **n**
sledge **n + v**
smell **n + v**
snack **n**
snowball **n**
snowboard **n**
snowman **n**
so **adv + conj**
soap **n**
soft **adj**
someone **pron**
somewhere **adv**
soon **adv**
sound **n + v**
sore **adj**
south **n**
space **n**
spaceship **n**
speak **v**
spend **v**
spoon **n**
spot **n**
spotted **adj**
spring **n**
stadium **n**
stamp **n**
station **n**
stay **v**
step **n**
still **adv**
stone **n**
storm **n**
straight on **adv**
strange **adj**
strawberry **n**

stream **n**
stripe **n**
striped **adj**
student **n**
study **v**
subject **n**
suddenly **adv**
sugar **n**
suitcase **n**
summer **n**
sure **adj**
surname **n**
surprise **n + v**
swan **n**
sweet(s) **n** (US candy)
swing **n + v**

T

take **v** (as in time e.g. it takes 20 minutes)
taste **n + v**
taxi **n**
teach **v**
team **n**
telephone **n**
tent **n**
thank **v**
theatre **n**
through **prep**
tidy **adj + v**
time **n**
together **adv**
tomorrow **adv + n**
tonight **adv + n**
torch **n** (US flashlight)
tortoise **n**
touch **v**
traffic **n**
trainers **n**
tune **n**
turn **v**
turn off **v**

turn on **v**
tyre **n**

U

umbrella **n**
unfriendly **adj**
unhappy **adj**
unkind **adj**
uniform **n**
university **n**
untidy **adj**
until **prep**
use **v**
usually **adv**

V

visit **v**
volleyball **n**

W

waiter **n**
warm **adj**
way **n**
west **n**
where **pron**
while **conj**
whisper **v**
whistle **v**
wife **n**
wifi **n**
will **v**
William **n**
win **v**
wing **n**
winter **n**
wish **n + v**
without **prep**
wood **n**
wool **n**

X

x-ray

Y

year **n**
yet **adv**
yoghurt **n**

Z

zero **n**